Per Diem

Per Diem

poems by

DAVID WEISS

TIGER BARK PRESS ✧ ROCHESTER, NEW YORK ✧ 2019

Published by Tiger Bark Press,
202 Mildorf Ave., Rochester, NY 14609.

Tiger Bark Press books are published by Steven Huff,
and designed by Philip Memmer.

Cover photograph by Lee Arthur Newell

The author wishes to thank the editors of *Nine Mile* for first publishing the poems "Hardening Up," "Late," "Equinox" and "Unreadiness."

ISBN-13: 978-1-7329012-2-3

Contents

For Bobbie

Its Own Season

Autumn in summer
The barn door hangs by a hinge

Someone's mother's smoking at the window
the life she never lived the life she is living

She's like the purple flowers   the ones
that outlast their leaves and seem to be levitating

Smoke's coming from a chimney nearby
and the mayoral race has turned nasty

Autumn in August
A milk snakes curls up in the folds of the silver tarpaulin

A log truck downshifts on the steep grade
Bees are working double time

There was midwinter spring once   that gift
Mid-stride   a fox freezes to take a sounding

These nights the stars brighten with cold
I'm just not going to get it done

Only the moon is steadfast
Most of the rest of us can only dream

Well water always has a chill
There's the one who comes and goes

without ever leaving
Close as I can get to it

The dream of a dreamless sleep
belongs to someone you'd least suspect it of

Pulling up stakes hurts even when it feels good
It isn't valedictory this nearness of the frost line

That red fox was more alive than the word *alive*
Crickets have gone brown   still springing

Close as I can get

Too Hot to Touch

Like bodies   walnuts fall   hard   irreversible
Apples drag their branches to the ground

But a cricket has come and changed the way I feel
Its slow wearing out makes an ungreased beautiful sound

Neither morning nor evening is a choice
not rain on the roof or the slow-mo wing-beat of the great blue heron

We can only let them happen   like my heart below your hand
Unmowed   the garden is like a stadium filled to capacity with heads
          of Queen Anne's lace

Hay bales blacken where the tarp doesn't cover them
She stood beneath the sun and wasn't certain if

she or the sun were the one who was going
Wasps swarm the windfall peaches

Whatever you can't prevent   you won't forget
I learned that from day one   back when no counting was needed

The rake that laid the hay in rows sits idle in the sun
its metal tines too hot to touch

When it came she knew it and stopped looking around
Even cows stand still when the lightning flashes   alert   newly speechless

Per Diem

Field stones pressed down all night
Trees stood erect on one foot
Over the meadow mist hovers in contused early light
And now the sun   its varnished glow
A wind is pushing before it the great necessities
Just as the morning glory has a mind of it own
she wants so much more
Already men are out ditching the road
Sunlight is going see-through
Roofs and gnarled trunks are given their own colors
with that mastery of letting each thing be itself
The first bees are on the clover
You can feel the heat building   coming as if from far off
To start is really to go on   no matter how it feels
The goldenrod is incandescing   self-lit
Some things you have to do are not a gift to anyone
Stones are almost warm to the touch
Into the night they'll still be giving off heat
What I wouldn't give

The Quick and the Blue

You can tell the crow isn't crowing
Like us it's either joking
sending an SOS   or a warning
Leaves are coloring up and falling
You wonder how the snapping
turtle ever got across the macadam
alive   Garter snakes curl up between
bales of rye   Mice nest in
the insulation   They aren't dumb—
like us there are forces beyond
their control   When you're nine
and told you're not worth a damn
you take it to heart   a life-long
argument you're bound to lose
The turkeys made it through summer
four of them did   out of ten
moving through the meadow single-
file   watchful as periscopes   The thing is
it helps to forget that you're being
hunted or found out or found wanting
Some breather from vigilance is needed
The hawks overhead   circling   are
in their element   adjusting to wind
shift and thermals   It's thrilling
to be quick on your feet   to roll with
the punches   to duck
the dark blur that streaks
in   out of the blue

Hard to Tell

For all the world it looks
as though the morning star
has fallen from the sky
to burn like a reading lamp
in someone's sitting room
The trees against the sky
are nubbed with buds
Like brightness   emptiness
starts somewhere
like the screeching you heard
last night   so near it felt
alarming   or else across
the field in the hedge row—
hard to tell   like how much
time you've got left
A light bulb's barely visible
once the sun comes up
heat baking the sky white
like a child you can't keep
from crying   Day starts
nonetheless   with the cool
sweet of hyacinth
the grass cool too   sweating
and the four horses slated
for the race track
and its narrow stalls
that come out into
the pasture a last time
to breath it in

A guy stands all day at
the big intersection in town
with a cardboard sign
that reads   *Hungry*
will work for food

In Spate

Wind blows through the trees
steady as a flautist's breath
Some bird starts up
with a trill and a chortle
that makes the woods
cavernous as outer space
No need   no need of me   no need
it says   Like a barrel
kicked on its side
I listen   Tree frogs
pipe up pure as a tuning fork
struck against the wrist

I was sent out   once upon a time
and lost my way
Here I am now   in an open doorway
Long into the night
the peepers are still giving it
everything they've got

As it Happens

Snow forecast   frost a day or two away
You lift a plank of wood and find spooled around itself   a snake
Up the hill a neighbor is felling trees
Just one maple in the midst of yellowing is going up in flames
The pile of drainage stone—you feel its inertia   its unwillingness
Clouds are closing in
The bees in their counting house are humming
Like the broken mower in the field I can't seem to finish what I've started
When no one's looking dust sifts down on the lamp and photo album beside it
A crow walks about like someone collecting empties by the side of the road
A second crow climbs the stone heap for the hell of it
The wheelbarrow has firewood in it   and water
On a shelf below the stairs apricot halves hang in syrup like jellyfish
Preparing has satisfactions the way readiness has illusions
So much starting that isn't beginning   so much ending that isn't finishing
The toad that crossed my path this morning will soon begin to dig
        its living grave
The yellowed leaves incandesce like a second sun
By end of day we'll sit and eat   side by side
But now rain comes down   slow at first   settling in

Clean Sweep

When the crickets start up you can begin counting the days
The mind belongs to no one   least of all itself
There's nothing you can do about that

When the story is over you know why she told it
The cat   the torn clothing   the crying in the night
the trees wild with wind

Even the driver isn't in the driver's seat
You'll lay this in the ground because where else can you put it:
those rows she dug   the seedlings   the boy it was for

What I'm saying is we all try like crazy
The corn in the field points insistently to the sky
If it's not the noon whistle chances are   it's fire

The problem with being angry is it makes a person stupid
When the last crickets stop their stridulations
you still can't tell where the hammering is coming from

Stupid means thinking it's one thing when it's many
Sun makes the ruts hard
What's next is something you aren't waiting for

All Night Rain

The all night rain is just getting to the bottom of the hill
The leaves of the ironwood tree stir only if you watch them

On the shelves books lean left or to the right
Nobody owns the words   which are like rain

I don't get what all the fuss is about
you open your hand   and it's gone

and then the hand and you too
are almost to the bottom of the hill

At the top of the hill it levels out
and doesn't feel like the top

There's always something lower than the bottom
You'll know it when you get there

If the kid gets more of the answers right   that's one life
If he doesn't   it's another

Still   it feels like the only life

Mine's winding down
At the bottom of the hill are houses

some old   some prefab   kids waiting for the bus
kicking stones

More rain's on the way
Mold blooms on the wood tabletop

Pills for the blood   pills for the heart
No pill for gravity   No pill for the shy smile

It's a long way to North Carolina if you're driving alone
and it's dark and the sky is falling

and the tires hiss and the radio station fades in and out
I'm with you in spirit

Rain is dripping from the eaves
These words could end up on the bookshelf if I put them there

or in a dumpster
on the way to the landfill

Same difference
though no one puts it that way

Lights Out

The springing heifer is dying   or giving birth
It's not clear which she is doing more of
Last night it was as if the stars were groaning
and today she still is
All night on her side in heavy rain
No one knows the trouble she's seen
My grandfather walked home by himself age six
after having his tonsils out
My grandmother called for him from her sickbed over and over
The sun keeps coming up later
One day it won't come up at all
and then love where will love be
For now the cicadas' glissando lifts us over the top
The blade of a sharpened scythe moves
like Ursa Major around the pole star
since before love knew what love is
One by one my grandfather shot the lights out
in the house as she cried his name
The faux grape vine has pulled the cherry tree
down to earth   taken its light
You put your shoulder to the wheel
Humming a blues also helps

Road Work Ahead

First you see one
Then a bee's on every head of clover

The news is coming
news that she won't be getting up

Small windowpanes don't break up the view
which out there is continuous

It's like what's under paint that's chipped off
Think how far back the sawdust goes

On the road
they're putting tar in the cracks to buy some time

I waited by the mailbox   you didn't come
Then I waited a little longer

The sun comes out for a second in a big way
then we're up against it again.

All these heads of Queen Anne's lace
like cake plates spinning on sticks

I'd always wanted to be decisive
And then it was decided

The trees are taking shallow breaths
in it for the long haul

#2 stone when you fill a hole with it
won't pack down

A coyote   the color of straw   moves
through the open field

It sees us   we don't see it
most of the time

When it's heavy   you need
both hands for each pull

Like the White-Throated Sparrow

A crow is having its say
and golden rod is having its
One of them sounds like a car alarm gone off

Sun behind this haze drills down
It eats at the mind
You'd rather not say aloud

what you know
unless you could say it
like the white-throated sparrow

Jewelweed's inflating its orange
windsocks   which hummingbirds love
A sunflower is slowly opening its eye

You were the kind of guy who
cracked a book in a darkened room
while jackhammers went at concrete

Women with small dogs waited for the light
You'd already lived   and now reliving
did what living had once done for you

There's no going uphill quietly
At the top's where the jewelweed grows
in shade along the ditch   So much work

is repair work   So much finding is
digging up   At night coy dogs lift their throats
and reinvent space itself

If you can't be good   be careful
If you can't be careful   be honest
If you can't be honest   be true

to the voice coming from the woods
where traps have been set
and the deer stand's high up in a tree

Burn Pile

On the burn pile a mockingbird
stood   flicking its tail   its nest
just under a splintered palette
I'd tossed on top along with
sacks the concrete had come in
as the stone walls went up
to make something square
and true and impervious
A groundhog poked out
from under the mound
where she'd dug a burrow
A rat snake sunned
on a torn black contractor bag.
Each bucket of stone we
hauled up the scaffold and fit
in place said *screw you* to
I didn't care who or what   I
went back down for more
from the incombustible pile.
Mocking chicks fledged
The burn pile grew   The walls
climbed higher than the poplars
we'd cut down   When the braces
iced up and mortar wouldn't
set   we closed up shop
doused the scrap with gasoline
as snow fell and wind swirled
the creatures gone by then
It went up fast into the bitter
air crackling with smoke
and crazy sparks   The sinews
in my twisting mind

crackled   too   and I
cursed with rabid joy
how things were
which I couldn't change
for all this building
that we'd take up again
in spring   the burn pile
spreading again like a thistle
patch and the mockingbird on it
imitating the sound of shovel
and hammer-drill
and pulley   as we hand-
over-handed the mortar up
to the top   all of it
good   You could see
the whole valley from the highest
point   and all of it
for all its unyielding rectitude
no damn good at all

Talk

In the freezer: two primals   bags of liver
tubes of ground beef   the big heart

Brownie's   who was never less than
a gentleman to the cows he pastured with

To the dragonfly you have no need to explain
To yourself you tell a different kind of lie

You touched your forehead
to the electric fence

A lifetime later
you opened your eyes

and had little to say
the trouble with having seen it all

She hasn't talked to you in weeks
but that's not why

you talk to yourself
up here in the hayloft

an archive of summer's sun and rain
and the baler's rhythmic work

stacked ten high
first through fourth cuttings

Orange twine you cut
to feed the cows waiting below

lies in a massive tangle
a kind of time piece

An uncle would take
the wire in one hand

and his brother's in the other
to give him a good jolt

too

When

When the engine died and I rolled onto the shoulder
and switched off the lights I heard it: the sky's silvery whispers
Shriveled leaves were swept into the air   like the future telling us
          a thing or two
A simple red cotton dress lay across the bed

Each time a fly dies   buzzing on its back   eternity suffers a tiny setback
Why stone cold to the touch offers comfort I don't really know
but when a vole takes its last rapid breaths
the tree nearest knows to bow its head

When she died she took us with her
Something will be eaten no doubt   a fiery thing downed
A great current sweeps before it all of us
who are trying to do better than just make do

Till then   there's the awful thump when a possum goes under the wheel
and those stores where the lights burn day and night
Miles of darkening air unfurl as evening falls
Without a doubt   it's clear   doesn't really mean that at all

Sometimes How Much   Sometimes How Many

Misery   like goldenrod   flowers long into the late season
A picture frame hangs crooked in the wood shed
A big limb on the Baldwin has cracked
sagging to the ground   dense with apples
Letters home have spilled on the dirt floor of the cellar
The big meat grinder unearthed   resembles a French horn
Sealed jars contain a brown substance that may once have been peaches
Here's a glass butter churn and next to it an illustrated history
of the Italian campaign—military field censor approved
Meat's in the freezer

In the pasture where calves grazed last year
gaudy orange pumpkin flowers
Against a hay bale a steer lies in the sun
A dam licks dry and soft with rough tongue its just-born
before she's taken away to the milk parlor
There's just suck and chew   and then another thing to do
Soy yellows right up to where the wall of corn starts
It's unabating the work   the odor of cut grass
of manure—sometimes earthy   sometimes too much

From the west clouds come swaying in like freshening cows
and lift sections of barn tin
A downspout's broken off halfway down
A hay wagon under cover is half-full   a tire flat
It's not just the fields that are harrowed and rolled
We don't get on   and still get on with it
Dead cows rise from the compost
whole   beside the making hay which timothy makes sweeter
Something about a filled hayloft makes one stop still
You can almost see the lake from up here
beyond the transfer station and the railroad tracks
Up here you're almost somewhere else

Morning After

The sun afterwards like forgetfulness
although icicles aren't melting
The sky has a blue mask on
Sparrows spill out like
notes that have left the stave
Wind played the chimney top last night
as though night were a bad idea
there was no getting away from
You sewed coats for the calves
to keep the shivering down
We shook more straw out for bedding
There's living   there's dying
it's how to live that's baffling
Sometimes sun's enough
Sometimes a shopworn word is
Sometimes the ice is so black
nothing keeps you standing
Yet the sparrows have a liveliness
that feels uncorked   like high spirits

Pear and Paver

The back-up beep of a dump truck
Asphalt comes out black and shiny as
a bear I watched cross a road and vanish
Was it an owl or a dog in pain last night   dying or just exulting
Roadwork has a cleanly smell like clothes in the dryer
The paver levels the tar   a steamroller takes the softness out
The electric fence ticks like a metronome   keeping time
When cracks again appear in the road
the cows masticating their hay won't be the same ones
nor will what's set us apart   The pear tree by the soy field
will have a lot of pears on it or just a few   Some
fall to the ground and soften early   Each day
you eat one or just part of one because there are more pears
than anyone can eat and fire wood to stack
and there's a limit to how much you can help   The pear
has such a clean pear-y taste if a little hard and woody
Ladder-tall late flowers are keeling over   big yellow heads
brushing the ground   You haven't been up the ladder yet
to sweep the chimney this autumn   The bald eagle
comes in low over the treetops heading
back to its nest   the paver is far down the road
The book beside the bed is so full of cares
and predicaments that   later   it will keep you
from your own for a while

Riding Down the Lake

You're not going far
Wind takes the last leaves

shoulders the bike sideways
The sun drops beneath the clouds

a reminder
the weird amber glow like sap

insects are preserved in
It's spitting rain

The wet road has a dark shine to it
You're not going that far

but you can't feel your fingers anymore
All you hear is the engine

and your own thoughts
which sound pretty much the same

Loud may as well be quietude
Cold may as well be the end of the line

A hay wagon sits empty beside a barn
The fields are all down to the ground

You lay low over the gas tank
This gale is lopping the tops off the waves

You're moving faster
yet even the next curve feels far away

Tomorrow's already happened
Yesterday is waiting in the wings

What was she thinking of
when she lost control of the wheel

Sunlight's horizontal now
Shadows can't stretch any farther

You'll only be getting *some* where
no further

Frayed   bruised-looking
picking up speed

the clouds are bottom-lit
as if light were coming up out of the earth

Ice keeps the trough from freezing solid
You break it with a shovel
so the steer can drink
Frozen to the ground last February
we couldn't get them out
till it thawed   By summer
they were rising to the top
of the compost heap
dug up by fox and coyote
Wind out of the north
won't relent or make apology
The ground so hard
he poured water over them
to case them in ice till spring
his eight-year-old   her mother
He carved their stones by candlelight
With the blossoms   countless of them
anger returns   and something else
The trough heater keeps it from icing
Cold steam comes off the surface
A cow will dip its muzzle
and draw water up
If the sky's clear tomorrow
mist will rise off the lake
and a long dark cloud
will blot out the sun

End of Dusk

In the west   a stone-washed sky above the inky trees
Grass gets damp as from great exertion
The blacktop I put my hand to is body temperature
Isn't that always the trick
The bees are in for the night
What the rest of us are doing I don't want to imagine
There's a dark so absolute nothing is beyond thought
Cicadas once insistent as the Ode to Joy
sound far off as the sea
The wrought iron rail also holds its heat
Fidelity can stay on the wing without landing only so long
You hear in the screech owl's soft braying
something needy it knows how to satisfy
Where you are now is near as a whisper I can't quite make out
There's a light across the valley   more than one
though one would be enough
and a man there who can't get up
or sleep   a vet   who lies in the dark
even after the birds start up   even after first light

Under Cover

Rain took the snow down
then the colors out   Mist
came up from the ground
The ground softened
and turned to mud   the
mud-colored horses stood
in the puddled field   stoic
placid   The damp was chilly
the day dim as a dirty window
and after doing this chore
and that   we got back under
the covers where it was humid
not damp   One thing led to
another   it felt good the way
when you were alone and in pain
and the pain wasn't going away
you'd groan softly with each breath
Sometimes someone came and you
could be quiet   less worried   her hand
on your forehead   the radiator
ticked as heat came up into it
The feeling of desolation subsided
Cold driving rain came down
outside the window   not in
and you felt safe   this was
why you were going to live
and also how when the time
came you'd be the one
waited for   who came with
cocoa and comfort and
certainty that it would be
all right   an illusion which lasts

just long enough
and helped you go on
and later to pass on
something about intimacy
Side by side   unmoving
in the downpour   the horses
breathe out warm white breaths

Either Way

The ash went down   stripping branches
from a bass tree   uprooting a maple
that started to keel over but hung up in an oak
Limbs thick as trees snapped as the ash hit down
Then it was silent   and he was still divorced
and the kids were never ready when he came
to pick them up Sundays
He'd cut the wedge out then made the hinge
The tree just stood there   before the carnage
of falling   as if nothing was changed
then it began to tip and come down and
then it was as if the woods had always been
as they were now   His mother was
dying of lung cancer four hours away
his girlfriend was expecting him later
Contrails in the opened sky overhead were
streaking by without a sound   who knew where

The trunk he sectioned into 16" lengths
It would take all day to get the wood out and split
He'd never get done if he didn't keep at it
It would be better if he didn't have to see
any of them again   he couldn't make them
happy   they wanted something from him
and he only wanted to be left alone
which like the maple leaner was not in the cards
He would have to cut it off above the roots
and pull it back with a chain until it slid
down or took the small oak with it   Either way

Unreadiness

A wagon train of clouds is trekking east
In the fields no rows are left for the fox to move through unseen
Blackberry shoots scratch at the window to get in
The cold rain stings
You can remember a thing only so long
Blue sky breaks through and pleases the eye
The water is cold   the trough scuzzy   but the cows don't mind it
They're in it for the duration   which is not all that long
Nothing welcoming in the air   ground hard underfoot
You like it outside where knuckles ache
and there's always another thing to get done
On the inside something's missing
The dog barks   he's going blind
Nor can the small plane up in the clouds see a thing
So much to get ready   to get ready for
If you close your eyes you can see her face
turning back   half-hidden by hair
And still you don't know how to find the tulip tree
once its leaves have blown away

Sun on Snow

A hard glare off the snow
You stop and close your eyes
You just want to stand there
You just want to be ravished
to let it take you over
The day began badly
an angry phone call   something
ruined by neglect
You couldn't settle   get undistracted
Now you just let it
It hurts it's so bright
You can see your own blood lit up
living redness and its laneways
It keeps brightening   the radiance
radiating   The snow on the field's
untouched   not a footprint on it   not
a paw   no leaf   no soot   no smudge
no was   You aren't anyone
you'd be disappointed in
or sorry to know   You stand there
your shadow behind you
You're not even thinking
of the cloud that will take it
all back and restore
a chill shrunken smallness
That may be the reason
you open your eyes and go on

Hardening Up

Yesterday sun branded your back
Today wind is roaring like the sea
Yesterday there was plenty of time
Today you can't even feel your toes
A buck lifts its head ready to bolt
Yesterday you'd stop to talk
Today snow careens sideways
and you're not looking up
Later the wood you split
will be going up the stove pipe
We are the birds that stay
is how she put it
though going wouldn't change a thing
Your letter said as much
One then two shots   far down the hill
and the buck is gone
You can survive getting lost
or lonely   if you don't lose your head
You can even survive the touch
that melted your heart

Late

The moon's a mole tunneling
through the sky   so cold
you can see its breath
You can hear creaking
in the trees which crack
without breaking   You're
out looking for a dog
that's missing   It's 2 am
and you've been calling
Now you're just walking
stopping   listening
Long ago
you found the dog
you were searching for
its front paw clenched
in a trap   Part-collie
it made a sound so soft
you didn't hear it
until you were beside her
Now each tiny snap
makes you listen harder
At the bee hives
you go close and
make out the sound of
ten thousand wings vibrating
like a choir in a cathedral
Really   what do you
know about anything   You'd
like to go back
in where the fire's warming
the walls   but a dog

is out there where
it's unforgiving   and
who knows what else

So Dense

Fog so dense headlights loom up suddenly near
There's just you and this clammy whiteness
like your father's squashed memory
He would stand stock still listening to what he'd never heard
or hearing what he'd never listened for
A dog barks close by   or far off   it's hard to say
I feed the shunned Guernsey a windfall apple
Her mind   squeezing out the juice   is in her mouth
By the end he took exception
By the end he made a point of reiterating the main points
By the end he couldn't be bothered   he washed his hands of it
Such primitive disgust with it all
This white hurts the eyes
White the future
What choice did he have but to take it personally   being a person
The Guernsey goes back to what there is   cropping grass
Even fog must cast a shadow   as the beloved dead do
White the future

In the Grip

The cheap solar-powered LEDs
stayed lit and made
a small circle of light
beneath the snow
as if someone bearing a torch
were headed underground
Snow was coming down heavy
and the sunken lights led
down to the darkened stone house
The snow was past his knees
Wind had erased the long path
he'd shoveled the week before
It would be years
before he'd lose his way
so thoroughly
that all trace of him
would be gone   Only if
you picked up a chisel
from the dusty workbench
would you feel in the wood
handle just how he
held it   loose but precise
and there he'd be—
in the grip

Allegory

Streamers jet from the unrisen sun
then shadows travel out   almost infinitely long
and window panes appear on the wall

a fiery orange
The clock that's been ticking all along
starts ticking in earnest

You ask me what I'm thinking   Is
watching a walnut limb bob—
feeling the weight of it—thinking?

To matter become conscious of itself
is anything nothing more
than what it is?

Put your ear to a bee box
and you'll be teased out of thought
I'm not thinking of you

exactly   but am aware
of your weight and warmth
beside me

and of your *so-much-ness*
which even as I reach for you
is getting out of bed

Bow Season

Men stand patient in the dark before the dark begins to lift
Oak holds on to its leaves   hickory doesn't   box elder doesn't
A bird chirps like a wheel with a bad ball bearing
Moving through the dark the deer are more alert than the men hunting them
Men are alert in the woods and in the bars
The women know this all too well—until they're lonely   on the rebound
How thin a twig end is
The sky's empty as a rinsed dinner plate
Later I'll recall what I'm too alert to think about
Later I'll remember who I think I am
The bird that cries bloody murder does so as evening falls
Half the time you're stiff   cold   half the time over a barrel
Eternity is shortened by anticipation
The arrow goes in till it hits bone
You follow the blood till the blood stops
though the breathing won't have
The trees seem to hold the sky up
What you do next requires
that you get down on your knees

Wintering Over

The moth outside on the thermopane
is an X-ray of a moth

double-winged   veined as a leaf
Snow falls past it

The spider   looming above
is just as dead

For heat we fight—
a feast of wrongs   a month of Sundays

Ash builds up in the stove
the meadow unyielding underfoot

Or else the moth
is riding out the cold

its four hair-legs
gripping glass

so perfectly inanimate
you'd hardly know

Sometimes all you ask for
is a little breathing space

and the verisimilitude
to get through it

Sparks

All night a warm wind
The ground has reemerged
like a land mass at the end
of an ice age   shocking
the *there-all-along* of it
At the cemetery gate
late one night a red fox
froze in the headlights
totemic   everything you'd lost
We laid stone up so high
we saw above the trees
the spatter of house lights
desolate before dawn
The burn pile   the unused stones
are clear of snow
the dirty bandage of it
And on the tip
of the highest branch
of the hickory in the meadow
a crow's perched   taking stock
You take what's given
the blow   the piece of luck
Torched   the burn pile
will melt stemware and throw
sparks into the black sky
until there is only
black sky

It

The long straightaway   ice-white
Every branch with its crust of snow
The sky on a bed of nails
Snow slants in   small and sharp as glass
The cow stands in it   steadily grinding hay
which still has the whiff of summer grass about it
I put my face to it as I fed it out this morning
heavy bales we stacked all summer in the barn
green and scratchy   the twine tight
The loft-door keeps slamming
an empty sound that is a searching sound
a not-finding sound   a sound
best listened to while rubbing oil
into leather or thinking of that skin
so crinkled and transparent
you found pressed between bales
where the snake had silently shed it
like clothes on the floor
and she   nowhere to be found

Declaration of Sentiments

The cow went down
by the feed trough
and couldn't get up
the concrete icy
her back legs splayed
temp below zero   the wind brutal
We braced her hooves
and urged her up
with prods and kicks
We put straw beneath her
and covered her with a tarp
until the sling could be gotten
to lift her with the skid steer
Other cows crowded close
They butted us   agitated
when we laid the tarp over her
I loved them for that
In the dry cow barn   heavy
and swaying   they'll cluster
around a new-born
to keep us at bay   A cow
will protect a calf
as if it were her own
Last summer when a just-born bull
wet from the licking off
still rocky on its pins
was carted off   a Holstein
herself ready to birth broke
through the fence into the road
to bellow inconsolably
as the trailer drove away
which didn't change a thing
but to make me feel amazed
and small

Misericordia

The rain's freezing as it comes down
Below the snow is more ice

She's near and then she's far
and then you can't be sure

where the present stops
and the past begins

You walk across the lake
following in the steps of a gray fox

Ervin Archibald lay for a day
tangled in weeds below your feet

till divers fished him out
He lay on shore

in a body bag   spent
You can still hear it

his friend who he'd saved
from drowning   howling

for help in the shallows
The ice is thick   the reeds sparse but tall

She's merged with the trees now
the trees darkened by rain

You have a fair idea
what it sounded like

You hope you never
have to make that sound

When it's made
you'll be so close by

you'll know
that help won't arrive in time

Breaker

The weather stripping leaks
The expansion tank's low on pressure
water just dribbling out
We've got the wood cook stove
stoked   just to keep up
Right now there's more night
than day   more *no* than *yes*
More *out of* than *in to*
The wind bites down
and doesn't let go

He had to shoot the deer
wedged under the car
to get it out
The couple who hit it
thought that cruel and unnecessary
He lay in the road
and stared at the splintered antlers
the one open panicked eye

No proof there's some day
in the night   some *yes* in *no*
more *into* in *out of* than you'd think
more love in getting by
more *now* in *then*
A dull maul splits wood just as well

You feel your way down to
the breaker box and flip the switch
The lights go back on

You can't see the snow
driving sideways now
just a dark reflection
going past the window

Three Over Twelve

The speed square booklet jammed
in the door jam keeps the wind quiet
The window glass has iced over
on the inside   snow still falling
as the light comes up blue and slow
like the mantle on a storm lantern
Sometimes it dawns on you that
this is your life   take it or leave it
What creature is so small
it hasn't fallen through this powdery snow
that sits like a top hat on the chair
you never put away back in October
A neighbor's beefers got out then
and knocked it and the motorcycle over
They shouldered scaffolding aside
Everything leaves a mark if you can read it
Whatever's low to the ground now is out of sight
The grill   a spade you forgot   some cans
of beer   will reemerge worse for wear
Cruelty can't be taken back
Gray-white   furry   a head pokes up
gone so quick   you might only
have imagined it through swirling snow
which shows no sign of letting up

Clear Cut

All the way to the trees snow fell
and all the way through them it fell
till we got to where they'd been
taken down carelessly   the big ones
skidded out   pine and poplar
and twenty-year oak   felled and left
every which way like matchsticks
It was ugly and denuding and when
the snow melted it would still be ugly
and the guy who owned it would still be
deep in debt and his wife still drifting
through the house on meds   a zombie
The long meadow between his windows
and where we stood couldn't disguise
the mess the loggers made and what for
All the way back through the trees
which belonged to another neighbor
it snowed   these useless woods
turkeys like for beech mast
and hunters for the turkeys and
the deer that nibble the growing
tips and rub their horns off on fallen
limbs and which the emerald ash borer
likes for the ash trees we take down
for firewood when their crowns thin
overhead and let in more and more light
each summer   which was far off and
not on either of our minds as the snow
fell workman-like and the stoical
trees dark against the white of snow
did what trees do

Still Time

It comes to you
before you can tell
power pole from ash tree
before you can
make out trees at all
You're waiting to hear
how it's turned out
It's not your life anymore
that matters
though you live it as you must
and relive it as you do
You've never stopped
being a fool
Now the shed roof's
come into view
and the combined rows
run wavery-straight
all the way to the poplars
No one's headed to work yet
that grind   nor has the corn
yet been ground to go
in the mixer
Before you hear it
you see the running lights
coming down the road
some someone   who could be
you   who had to get away
and snaps the radio on
then off   preferring
the wide dirty sky ahead
and what it feels like

to choose nothing
over something
to have thrown it all away
and yet still have time—
while his son and daughter
moist mouths agape   lie
sleeping through the sun's
silent   splendid
coming up—still time to
turn back and walk in the door
like nothing happened
just out getting milk
The car barrels past
You go outside to
set the gate back on its hinge posts
It's the rattle of the latch
catching   that does it
as you swing it to
The gate keeps nothing
in or out
You open and close it
nonetheless
as you wait for word

Elision

The stars were dead if bright meant dead
and the golden rod was dead
if gray in the wind and stiff meant dead
The shovel in my hands went in
It thought nothing of the hole that grew
Both shovel and hole were dead
The dog that went in looked alive
and the girl who stood in the star-dark
didn't cry   alive to the murmuring air
immense and empty   that washed
over our standing there as the shovel
did its moving work   the dog
indifferent to the dirt that rose around it
Then a piece of the moon also rose
and it was deadest of all   beautiful
and votive and touch-me-not   goodbye-alive
And we were done   if done means
never done and touch-me-not means
touch me

Unseasonal

Unseeable the trees through the falling snow
just a darker white   a paler dark
and the snow coming steady like time made visible

You went toward the sound
that hadn't anything to do with trees or snow
It was like time made audible

time at the mercy
of a deeper   sharper time
that pinned it down to take its life

It was a fox very much alive
in the ruddy throes
of a drive I felt in the glands of my throat

that led to every mistake I'd made
but I knew just one thing
while a fox knows many

And she was gone
snow no obstacle
into the trees beyond sight

No one would witness
the undressing
though you could find the spot

if you tracked the pale red drops
like so much red wine
the snow so much like oblivion

Unheimlich

The cold
makes your eyes tear   your nose run

It makes your hands stiff
It gets in your bones

but the horse needs water
a car has to be pulled from the ditch

you've got to find the short
and where the pipe's cracked

The stars are acetylene bright
You can smell their clean dead breath

Stalks sway without bending
You turn your back

and hook the chain around the axle
You'd call it quits but you can't

Your face is numb   but you keep moving
There's no philosophy in it

or triumph of the will
You may as well ask a dray horse

why it keeps going
All you can say is

the rain gutter that's pulled loose
whangs with each gust

And there is the Pleiades
which you can't help

but notice in the east
its dense faint scatter

that's beautiful
but offers no fellowship

A Little Something

You once knew a little
something about soft spring air
and what it does

You knew about
tree peepers   crocuses   not
taking no for an answer

The sooty snow mounded high
in the Lowe's parking lot
looks like it won't ever melt

Each time you squeeze a lemon
or tighten the fence wire
the cracks in your fingertips

remind you   Each time
you put your fingers
in a calf's warm wet mouth

to be sucked
you recall those alarming
thrills and what ardor is

and stand in the stall
the calf quiescent
resurrecting

Stock Still

The calves you bottle-fed last night
didn't yet know how to suck
Then they did

Their eyes rolled back in their heads
They jerked   kicked
Jacketed   they lay down in straw

to ride out the cold
which couldn't be kept out
Most will survive it

The ones that don't will
be dragged out by the hocks
and slung into the manure truck

The cold gets in you
the wind's an engine revved
too high   At your wit's end

there's no one you don't hate
no one who's not to blame
Work—one emergency after another

Now a high caul of cloud   blued-through
Snowmobile tracks   bobcat prints
all but wind-blurred

Sun's the sign of cold
a huckster you believe in
in spite of yourself

The coffee's bitter but hot
A cow's down
the hoof trimmer's coming

You've no time to take stock
You'd like to go out
when something tells you

you're ready
A snow-devil races
along the frozen ground

as you step out the door
It twirls up and is gone
lovely   inimitable   a fellow traveler

Cold to the Touch

Out of the blue it's weirdly warm
Sun muscles through the breeze
to lay a hand on your cheek
Your heart breaks from your chest
For minutes at a time
you're animal not mineral
and want to
bound through the woods
like the dog that went off
chasing deer
The stone-hard ground
is halfway to mud
Before your eyes snow's retreating
though nothing's green
under it
not even a snowbell shows itself
The metal fence posts are
cold to the touch
                    They are all
crowding round you now
like they've never been gone—
tormenter, pals, beloved.
This is their afterlife
this surprise of nearness
you their underworld
until the sun goes down
and the ground that's sodden
a dark dark brown
freezes over   and you're back
among the footprint makers
who   once—you'd failed to realize—
saved you   though you

could not save them
Too slow to catch up
the dog makes its way home
long after dusk

Equinox

Like that
carousels of snow geese
out of the north
boomeranging in midair
black blurry wingtips dizzying
to us earthbound ones who'd
crawled out from under
the International Harvester
dragging the starter motor
whose brushes were too shot
to start anything   We stood cold-
toed and runny-nosed beneath that
feathered machine turning like Ezekiel's
wheels within wheels   and which
turned which we couldn't tell   They
banked dark against white cloud
white against blue sky
and the starter   too worn to
work   pulling our arms
down as rooted to the spot
we wheeled with the gyro-ing geese
that rose and fell off to weave
through each other like line
dancers or circus jugglers
spontaneous and intricate
unorchestrated and interlocked
With our eyes we took our best
shot and rode the revolving
kaleidoscope into a whooping
larger life where feeling sight
flung us until we couldn't hold it
up much longer and lugged

the iron thing like a passel of geese
to the bed of the pickup
then on to Monroe Tractor
to order a rebuilt
the sound of the honking still
geysering behind us as though nothing
mattered more than the pure
urgency of that commotion
which set us straight till our own
motion carried us to care
more for that kingdom of small
concerns we were headed toward
Our hands warmed in the cab
and fiery windblown minds turned
to incandescent and neon light
where by then a small hand
would seize hold of a forefinger
and tug it toward some other miracle
saying   *Daddy!   look!   look!   look!*

Thaw

Ditches ran and the gutters dripped
You couldn't see it happening—
the snow melting into snow
till milkweed stalk and bare bush
emerged and green-gray earth
in low spots by the fence posts
Sun bore down and the white
crust glittered and blinded
the whole hard winter of
frozen wind and glassy-eyed
calves dead in their home-
made coats   Horses took
long pulls from the clear trough
water pooled in muddy ruts
and the song running through
my head like a tire out of round
liquified in the general rout and
ran out toward the cockeyed stones
of the long dead who sloughed
their names and rose up into
the unindebted light   We'd been
hanging on for dear life   Now
you could feel it   this thing
a glee that made the squirrels
scrabble clockwise up a tree
in hot pursuit and down
just because—the only answer
there was—the only one
worth giving

Elsewhere

for Clea

Night followed day
the way I followed you through the market
the ten thousand shoes and shelled beans
the heaps of onion and cassava and fluttery fabrics
night siamesed to day
and day walking the paths between potato mounds
to where sweet milk waited
and cordiality and the boy Ruta gnawing a stalk of sugarcane
night was rain and stars and muffled sobs
and day was women and boys with water and baskets on their heads
and grass for the cows in their covered pens
and everyone asking each other come day if they still existed
which they did with a certainty borne of amazement
and the dazed men who were night in day drinking beer
and the women fetching water
and the bananas small and fat and lemony
and it's true that everyone walks behind each other
as day does with night and night with day

About the Author

DAVID WEISS is the author of a novel, *The Mensch*, and three collections of poems most recently *Perfect Crime* (Nine Mile Press). He co-edits *Seneca Review*, teaches at Hobart and William Smith Colleges, and lives on a farm in the Finger Lakes.

Colophon

The text of *Per Diem* is set in Adobe Garamond Pro.

This trade edition was printed by BookMobile in Minneapolis, MN.
26 copies were lettered and signed by the author,
for presentation purposes.
This copy is number:

Publication of this book was made possible
through the generous contributions of the following donors:

Laure-Anne Bosselaar
The Bishop Butler Society
Thor Gilbert-Huff
Stephen Kuusisto
Wendy Mnookin

More Poetry from Tiger Bark Press

Boy on a Doorstep, by Richard Foerster

Totem: America, by Debra Kang Dean

After Morning Rain, by Sam Hamill

Meditation Archipelago, by Tony Leuzzi

Fancy's Orphan, by George Drew

Translucent When Fired, by Deena Linett

Ask Again Later, by Nancy White

Pricking, by Jessica Cuello

Dinner with Emerson, by Wendy Mnookin

As Long As We Are Not Alone, by Israel Emiot,
translated by Leah Zazulyer

Be Quiet, by Kuno Raeber, translated by Stuart Friebert

Psalter, by Georgia Popoff

Slow Mountain Train, by Roger Greenwald

The Burning Door, by Tony Leuzzi

I've Come This Far to Say Hello, by Kurt Brown

After That, by Kathleen Aguero

Crossing the Yellow River, translated by Sam Hamill

Night Garden, by Judith Harris

Time-Bound, by Kurt Brown

Sweet Weight, by Kate Lynn Hibbard

The Gate at Visby, by Deena Linett

River of Glass, by Ann McGovern

Inside Such Darkness, by Virginia Slachman

Transfiguration Begins at Home, by Estha Weiner

The Solvay Process, by Martin Walls

A Pilgrim into Silence, by Karen Swenson